When the Earth
TREMBLES

An Engineer Looks At Earthquakes From A Christian Perspective

PAUL A. FAST

WinePress Publishing
MUKILTEO, WA 98275

To my Mother, whose assistance was invaluable

CONTENTS

CHAPTER ONE

EARTHQUAKE!

"It was the evening of November 23, 1980. My husband, our three sons, several relatives and I were gathered in the family home in Avellino, Italy. Suddenly we felt a strong gust of wind. Then everything began to move. The house rocked like a ship on the high seas. We heard buildings collapsing around us and immediately recognized that it was an earthquake. As we crowded behind the jammed door, we realized there was no escape. We screamed for help. I cried out to the saints and to God for help, without knowing if they could hear me. As the earth shook, I felt I was about to appear before God....

After the main tremor, we managed to open the door. Before us lay the ruins of four collapsed apartment blocks with 87 victims buried beneath the rubble. Everything seemed so vain...." [1]

—*Esterina Candela*

This eyewitness account represents the agonizing experience of people who have survived one of many major earthquakes during the course of history. In this particular instance, the seismic shock that struck the Appenine Mountains in southern Italy claimed about 5000 lives and left about 200,000 people homeless. Almost every Italian village over an area of 10,000 square miles was reduced to ruins—including parts of the provinces of Naples, Avellino, Salerno, and Potenza.[2] The shifting of millions of tons of the earth's mass is a unique and overwhelming demonstration of sheer power and energy. It has been estimated that the energy released by an earthquake may be 10,000 times as great as that of the first atomic bomb.[3] There are no natural occurrences which happen with greater suddenness and cause more immediate widespread destruction than that of a major seismic event.

A few statistics of some of the major documented earthquakes will illustrate the enormous power and devastation unleashed by earthquakes and their ability to expose our lack of preparedness.

In 1556, Shensi Province in China experienced an earthquake in which an estimated 830,000 people died.[4]

In 1755, on All Hallows' Day, November 1, Lisbon, Portugal, one of the richest and most powerful cities of the day was rocked by three powerful jolts. A tsunami (tidal wave) followed, swallowing the people seeking refuge on the shores. The giant wave raced across the Mediterranean, devastating the coastal areas. In Madeira, the sea rose by 50 feet; lakes and rivers throughout western and central Europe churned; and ships as far away as Southampton, England, were torn from their moorings. Various reports put the death toll at 20,000 to 50,000 people.[5]

In 1811 and 1812, earthquakes centred under the Mississippi Valley in the central United States were felt as far away as Canada, New Orleans and the Atlantic seaboard.

More recently, on July 28, 1976, an earthquake jolted China. The city of Tangshan was completely destroyed. It is estimated that 500,000 people died.[6]

The most powerful earthquake in recent memory occurred in Anchorage, Alaska, on Good Friday, March 27, 1964. The quake exceeded 8.0 on the Richter scale. Since this area is sparsely populated, only 131 people lost their lives. The harbor and some buildings dropped 30 feet and, in some places, the land rose by 33 feet. A tsunami 50 feet high swept across the Pacific Ocean a distance of 8400 miles at a speed of 450 miles per hour. Slabs of soil and buildings were moved a quarter of a mile from their original locations.[7]

On October 17, 1989, the Richter magnitude 7.1 Loma Prieta earthquake struck San Francisco and the surrounding area. As a structural engineer interested in the response of buildings during earthquakes, I visited the damaged zone within days of the initial tremor and viewed the collapsed buildings and bridges, buckled sidewalks, burnt houses, and temporary shelters that were erected for the homeless. Although this would not be considered a major seismic occurrence, it became abundantly evident to me from the widespread damage that the world's large cities situated in earthquake-prone areas are extremely vulnerable to the catastrophic consequences of earthquake forces, particularly cities with many older buildings.

On January 17, 1995, the industrial city of Kobe, Japan, was hit by an earthquake of magnitude 7.0 on the Richter scale, resulting in roughly 5000 casualties, $200 billion of damage, 88,000 destroyed buildings and 300,000 homeless. One newspaper headline read, "With thousands dead and more missing, a nation at risk takes a chilling second look at its quake-proofing measures and wonders: What if it had been Tokyo?" Following the collapse of the Hanshin Expressway, a safety expert said: "We had a firm belief that highways were safe."[8]

The horror of such seismic events caused the internationally renowned architect Frank Lloyd Wright to comment: "There may be [a] more awful threat to human happiness than an earthquake—I do not know what it can be."[9]

In the early 1900s, Wright gained firsthand experience in earthquakes after having been commissioned to design the Imperial Hotel in Tokyo as an earthquake-resistant building. He was aware how earthquake prone Japan was: "There was this natural enemy to all building whatsoever, the temblor. And, as I well knew, the seismograph in Japan is never still."[10]

While visiting the site during the construction of the building, he experienced a series of lighter tremors. Finally, just prior to completion of construction, the strongest seismic shock to jolt the earth in the preceding 52 years occurred. It was a terrifying experience. This is how he described it: "A moment's panic, and hell broke loose as the wave motion began. The structure was literally in convulsions."[11] Frank Lloyd Wright was also keenly aware of the wide-ranging, disastrous effects of seismic upheavals: "After the irresistible wave movements have gone shuddering and jolting through the earth, changing all overnight in immense areas, islands disappearing, new ones appearing, mountains laid low and valleys lifted up taking awful toll of human life, then come the flames!"[12]

Two years after he returned to America, on September 1, 1923, a massive, magnitude 8.3 earthquake struck Japan's

Kanto/Tokyo district. Whole areas of land were moved and the entire island of Ooshima shifted 13 feet to the north. Forests slid into the water and homes were destroyed. In the process, the traditional cooking pots were overturned, causing a fire that raged for three days and gutted 65% of Tokyo's buildings. An estimated 140,000 people died. However, the Imperial Hotel did not collapse, nor was it destroyed by fire. Frank Lloyd Wright had incorporated into his design a big pool, which provided water to keep the flames at bay. The rest of Tokyo burned because the water mains had been disrupted by the quake.[13]

The people familiar with such feelings of fear are naturally those who live in areas that have been prone to regular earthquake activity—the so-called *Ring of Fire*, which consists of the coastal areas surrounding the Pacific Ocean, and the string of mountain ranges stretching from the East Indies, the Himalayas and the Caucasus mountains through Turkey, the Carpathians, the Alps, the Apennines of Italy, and reaching through Spain and Portugal down to the Atlas mountains of North Africa.

It is estimated that the world experiences an average of one major earthquake of magnitude greater than Richter 7 every 3 weeks and at least one moderate earthquake every 3 days. Every day, seismographs detect an average of almost 300 earthquakes of Richter magnitude 3 or greater. In light of this constant shaking, the earth can truly be described as a continually trembling mass of elements.

Searching to Understand

In response to this ever-present danger, no small number of philosophers have pondered the significance of such events, and why and how they occur. What causes the earth's crust to move and heave and cause such havoc? Are earthquakes just random natural occurrences? Do they represent the judgment of an angry God? Will they get worse?

Thousands of geoscientists, seismologists, and engineers have invested countless years of their time researching the technical aspects of this phenomenon—formulating theories about the cause of quakes, constructing laboratory-size "shaking tables" with model buildings that simulate seismic motion, and establishing earthquake-resistant design criteria.

Tremendous progress has been made in this field of endeavor. However, one goal of such efforts has remained disturbingly elusive, namely, the development of reliable earthquake prediction. In 1974, there seemed to be a startling success in earthquake prediction when, on February 4, 1975, Chinese authorities correctly predicted an earthquake and evacuated the city of Haicheng. An earthquake of 7.3 on the Richter scale struck the city, demolishing 90% of the buildings, but very few lives were lost. The Chinese had marshalled an army of 100,000 earthquake watchers who were monitoring such signs as strange animal behavior, swelling of the ground, foreshocks, changes in electric conductivity, and geomagnetics. Indeed, the area had experienced several 5.0 magnitude foreshocks in the preceding hours.[14] Some earthquake watchers were jubilant, for it seemed the time of pinpoint, accurate prediction was at hand.

Then a mere 17 months later, on July 27, 1976, an earthquake struck the city of Tangshan, China. Unannounced by any precursors, an estimated 500,000 people died, and twenty square miles of cityscape were turned into one giant heap of rubble.[15]

Based on research and the history of recorded earthquakes for the past 500 years, we now have a better understanding of which areas of the earth may experience greater earthquake activity. However, we cannot pinpoint the location and cannot predict the year, the day, and the hour of an earthquake. Charles F. Richter, after whom the Richter scale was named, once said: "Only fools, charlatans, and liars predict earthquakes."[16]

Finding Peace of Mind

It is true that by selecting a building site on bedrock and away from fault lines, avoiding building on landfills which are notorious for their instability, and by implementing earthquake-resistant construction, one can reduce the risk of destruction and thereby experience a certain measure of "peace of mind." Yet when we consider the vast, incomprehensible storehouse of energy that can be released in an earthquake—power that can literally move islands or mountains, as happened in the Kansu earthquake in China in 1920—isn't such peace of mind quite fragile against the backdrop of reality?[17]

Exploring and researching the geology and behavior of the earth will not ultimately provide us with satisfying answers concerning the *why* and *how* of this subject. Instead, I would like to suggest that we explore the ancient book known as the Bible in order to gain a better understanding of this phenomenon called *earthquake*.

One might ask, "Why study the Bible to understand earthquakes?"

First, it contains numerous reports and prophetic pronouncements concerning earthquakes, which provide us

13

with considerable insight into the perplexing questions surrounding this subject. Furthermore, it is the most widely read and influential book in history. More copies of the Bible have been distributed than any other book, and it has been translated into more languages than any other book. It is rich in ancient historical accounts, such as the creation of the world, the history of Israel, and the life of Christ. These accounts span centuries, yet all of them exhibit remarkable cohesiveness and harmony. Above all, the Bible offers a realistic view of human life and has provided untold millions of people with comfort, hope, and guidance during times of catastrophe and uncertainty.

The reader will find not only factual historical accounts of earthquakes in the Bible as well as prophetic announcements concerning future events, but will also discover some interesting technical insights. Those who are in sincere pursuit of truth regarding this subject and are seeking true peace of mind will be delighted to find, woven into the fabric of biblical earthquake references, a revelation of the power, wisdom, and majesty of our Creator and His great love for humanity.

CHAPTER TWO

EARTHQUAKES IN THE OLD TESTAMENT

F ive earthquakes, all with rather unique consequences, are mentioned in the Old Testament of the Bible. They occurred before the birth of Christ.

Mount Sinai

The first mention we find in the Bible of anything resembling an earthquake occurred in the early history of Israel when the entire Israelite nation was gathered at Mount Sinai—an 8,000-foot mountain, traditionally thought to be located in the southeastern region of the Sinai peninsula. This was a stopover for the people on their way from Egypt to their new homeland in Palestine. We read in the Book of Exodus:

On the morning of the third day there was thunder and lightning, with a thick cloud over the mountain, and a very loud trumpet blast. Everyone in the camp trembled. Then Moses led the people out of the camp to meet with God, and they stood at the foot of the mountain. Mount Sinai was covered in smoke, because the Lord descended on it in fire. The smoke billowed up from it like smoke from a furnace, the *whole mountain trembled violently,* and the sound of the trumpet grew louder and louder. Then Moses spoke and the voice of God answered him. (Exodus 19:16–19)

Subsequently, Moses received the Ten Commandments from God. Obviously this description differs from our usual understanding of the events surrounding an earthquake in that "smoke billowed up from it," and there were increasingly louder trumpet blasts. Reference is also made to thunder and lightning.

It is known that earthquakes can generate incredibly loud noises, often resembling the roar of thunder. Furthermore, it is also known that volcanoes are commonly situated in active earthquake zones, such as the Ring of Fire surrounding the Pacific Ocean. The movement of rock masses in the earth's crust results in tremendous heat buildup and, ultimately, volcanic activity. In this instance, it would appear that this movement resulted in a concurrent shaking of the mountain and "billowing of smoke."

Until recently, some skepticism prevailed among seismologists with respect to earthquake lights. During the Idu, Japan, earthquake of 1930, the Japanese seismologist Kinkiti Musya received nearly 1,500 accounts from eyewitnesses describing various kinds of lights. However, this phenomenon defies explanation. As one seismologist put it: "Earthquake lights constitute the darkest chapter in the history of seismology."[1]

Obviously such flashes of earthquake lights must have instilled great fear in the Israelites. Of primary significance to our discussion, however, is the fact that subsequent Bible references make mention of the *shaking* of the mountain. For example:

> The mountains *quaked* before the Lord, the One of Sinai.... (Judges 5:5)

> The earth shook...Sinai itself was moved at the presence of God... (Psalms 68:8 NKJV)

The inference from these verses is that the trembling and shaking of Sinai is an event the Jewish people did not forget and, in fact, used as a source of encouragement— remembering it as evidence of the strength and power of their God. Some 1500 years later, direct reference to this Sinai occurrence is also made in the New Testament Book of Hebrews:

> At that time His voice shook the earth, but now he has promised, "Once more will I shake not only the earth, but also the heavens." (Hebrews12:26)

The context surrounding this verse clearly refers to the frightening experience the Israelites lived through at Mount Sinai and shows how the trembling of this mountain was permanently etched into their memory.

Earthquake Swallows Korah

A further account of seismic activity in the history of Israel is found in the Book of Numbers, where we read about several Israelites who were challenging the authority of their leader, Moses, during their journey from Egypt to their new homeland in Palestine. In response, Moses ordered all the people to move away from the rebels.

> Then Moses said: "This is how you will know that the Lord has sent me to do all these things and that it was not my idea: If these men die a natural death and experience only what usually happens to men, then the Lord has not sent me. But if the Lord brings about something totally new, and the earth opens its mouth and swallows them, with everything that belongs to them, and they go down alive into the grave, then you will know that these men have treated the Lord with contempt."
>
> As soon as he finished saying all this, *the ground under them split apart* and the earth opened its mouth and swallowed them, with their households and all Korah's men and all their possessions. They went down alive into the grave, with everything they owned, *the earth closed over them* and they perished and were gone from the community. (Numbers 16:28–33)

The renowned Jewish historian Josephus, expanding on this account in his work *Antiquities of the Jews* some 1500 years later, wrote:

> When Moses had said this, with tears in his eyes, the ground was moved on a sudden; and the agitation that

set it in motion was like that which the wind produces
in waves of the sea. (IV.33)

This undulating movement of the ground has been lik-
ened to rolling sea waves by many earthquake survivors.
Seismologists call them *secondary waves*, as opposed to *primary waves*, which are characterized by a sudden, jarring
motion. In the minds of generations of Jewish people who
followed after Moses, this event was remembered as one
very much resembling an earthquake.

That the earth literally splits apart, *swallows up*, and
closes again is something history has shown to be character-
istic of other quakes as well. Sir Charles Lyell reported that
during the strong Calabrian earthquakes of 1783, houses
sank into great fissures, and the ground closed over them.
During the same earthquake, some men were said to have
fallen into the earth, only to be thrown out again.[2] Such
stories have been disputed by some. However, in the great
Fukui earthquake of June 28, 1948, there was clear evidence
of a woman falling into a crevice up to her chin and being
crushed to death.[3]

The fact that the sudden disappearance of Korah and
his people through such extraordinary means occurred after it had been foretold by Moses was an event which the
nation of Israel—like the shaking of Mount Sinai—never
forgot.

In the New Testament, Jude referred to this incident in
order to reinforce his warning against rebellious and corrupt leaders and their followers within the Christian church.
We read in the Book of Jude:

> In the very same way, these dreamers pollute their
> own bodies, reject authority and slander celestial

beings…they have been destroyed in Korah's rebellion. (Jude 8–11)

In other words, a similar fate, figuratively speaking, awaits corrupt religious leaders and individuals of the Christian church.

Israelites Saved by Earthquake

The First Book of Samuel records the following incident in which the earth shook. A small Israelite army of 600 men was being threatened by the Philistine army, which numbered 30,000 chariots and 60,000 horsemen. Clearly it was no match. The Israelites were so frightened that they hid in thickets, rocks, and pits. We then read:

> There was trembling in the camp, in the field, and among the people. The garrison and the raiders also trembled; *and the earth quaked* so that it was a very great trembling….And there was the multitude, melting away….so the Lord saved Israel that day. (1 Samuel 14:15, 16, 23 NKJV)

In this instance, the shaking of the ground produced a panic in the Philistine army. They fled, and Israel was saved from its enemy. It is interesting that an important message of our modern earthquake response program is: Don't Panic! Obviously this advice can be most difficult to heed in light of the tremendous forces at work during an earth tremor.

Elijah and the Earthquake

We read of another earthquake in the Bible which occurred when the Jewish prophet Elijah was hiding in a cave. He was fleeing from the king who sought to kill him. He was also deeply depressed over the lamentable spiritual condition of his king and his fellow Israelites.

> The Lord said, "Go out and stand on the mountain in the presence of the Lord, for the Lord is about to pass by." Then a great and powerful wind tore the mountains apart and shattered the rocks before the Lord, but the Lord was not in the wind. After the wind there was an *earthquake,* but the Lord was not in the earthquake. After the earthquake came a fire, but the Lord was not in the fire. And after the fire came a gentle whisper. (1 Kings 19:11–12)

The context of this passage indicates that the display of these three powerful forces—the wind, earthquake, and fire—remind Elijah that his God is still in control. It also symbolizes the threefold judgment pronounced in the following verses; judgment not directed toward Elijah but rather intended for his fellow Israelites who have rejected God. The *whisper* foreshadows God's mercy, which will shield and uplift Elijah and the remaining faithful believers within Israel.

Mount of Olives Earthquake

The last reference to an earthquake in the Old Testament of the Bible has both historical and prophetic significance. It is found in the Book of Zechariah, where we read:

Then the Lord will go out and fight against those nations as He fights in the day of battle. On that day His feet will stand on the Mount of Olives, east of Jerusalem, and the Mount of Olives will *be split in two from east to west, forming a great valley, with half the mountain moving north and half moving south.* You will flee by My mountain valley, for it will extend to Azel. You will flee as you fled from the *earthquake* in the days of Uzziah king of Judah....(Zechariah 14:3–5)

In this prophecy, the inhabitants of Jerusalem are depicted as being under siege by surrounding armies. While many will be captured, the Mount of Olives will split in two and create an escape route for some of the people.

Dr. Amos Nur, a Stanford University professor who has studied the history of earthquakes in Palestine, suggests that the earthquake at the time of King Uzziah occurred in 756 B.C. and destroyed parts of Jerusalem, Jericho, and other cities. He also states:

The most remarkable thing about this quotation from Zechariah is the clear description of a strike-slip fault in which the part to the east moved to the north and the part to the west on which we stand moved to the south. This is exactly the kind of motion that we know happens on the Dead Sea transform during earthquakes and is also the motion that we know involves plate tectonics as we know it today.[4]

In other words, the direction of the predicted earthquake is consistent with the natural fault line in this area.

We also notice that earthquakes cause the ground to not only split open and close again, but that they can also separate and move a huge mass of earth. This passage describes the movement of an entire mountain, splitting and keeping it apart, and thus creating a wide valley. Obviously, a similar event in the days of Uzziah was of such significance that it left a lasting imprint on the minds of the prophet and all Israel.

Massive earth movements happened in the Kansu, China, earthquake on December 16, 1920. One peasant woke up in the morning and was shocked to see that a high hill had moved onto his homestead, stopping just a few feet from his hut. Whole sections of roadway were transported across country. One roadway was lifted up, carried along for nearly a mile, and then set down complete with trees and the birds' nests in their branches![5]

This is a vivid reminder of what Jesus said to His disciples:

> "If you have faith as small as a mustard seed, you can say to this mountain, 'Move from here to there' and it will move." (Matthew 17:20)

Zechariah's prophecy indicates that God moves and splits mountains, if necessary, to provide an escape for people.

Other Old Testament Events

It has been suggested that other events described in the Old Testament of the Bible were also triggered by earthquakes. Such occurrences include the collapse of the walls of Jericho, when the Israelites marched around the city, and the parting of the waters of the Red Sea.

The Bible does not mention what made the walls of Jericho collapse, other than that it happened after the Israelites had been marching around the city for seven successive days and, on the last day, began to shout aloud with the priests blowing their trumpets.

Archaeological excavations of Jericho—which has been rebuilt numerous times—as well as historical accounts of earthquakes in Palestine appear to indicate that Jericho has been destroyed by earthquakes. In fact, as we have already seen, God often uses the forces of nature to accomplish his purposes. It would seem reasonable to conclude that the walls of Jericho were brought down by an earthquake on this occasion, but it would also be overly presumptuous of us to state this as a fact. God's means of executing His purposes are infinite and beyond comprehension.

As for the parting of the Red Sea, the contention that landslides triggered by earthquakes parted the water— thereby creating dry ground for the Israelites—runs contrary to the record of the Bible.

> And all that night the Lord drove the sea back with a strong east wind and turned it into dry land. The waters were divided,...with a wall of water on their right and on their left. (Exodus 14:21)

A similar occurrence happened in Canada in the not so distant past.

> On the night of March 28, 1848, Niagara Falls went dry....The explanation for this curious and frightening episode was fascinating. Heavy westerly winds flowing across Erie, the shallowest of the Great Lakes, had driven the bulk of its water over the Falls. Then the winds changed. Much of the water that was left was forced back far to the west. The wind also broke up the ice, which

formed a jam in the river near Buffalo, effectively damming it until only a trickle ran between the banks. When the ice jam broke and the wind dropped, the Falls returned to their former glory.[6]

We can trust God's Word. When God specifies a particular method by which He accomplished His purpose, then we may be certain that it happened exactly that way.

CHAPTER THREE

EARTHQUAKES IN THE NEW TESTAMENT

I n the New Testament of the Bible, four earthquakes are mentioned. They all occurred after the birth of Christ.

Crucifixion

The first occurrence takes place immediately following the crucifixion of Christ.

> And when Jesus had cried out again in a loud voice, He gave up His Spirit. At that moment the curtain of the temple was torn in two from top to bottom. *The earth shook and the rocks split...*when the centurion and those with him who were guarding Jesus saw the earthquake and all that had happened, they were terrified and exclaimed, "Surely He was the Son of God!" (Matthew 27:50–51, 54)

In order to appreciate the gravity of this event and understand the final exclamation of the onlookers, it is helpful to study the context. Before His crucifixion, Jesus endured endless ridicule and scorn despite having healed the sick; raised the dead; freed demonically-possessed persons; and having showed love, kindness, and goodness to many. He also had claimed to be the Son of God and the world's Messiah, speaking authoritatively about the need for all people of all races to repent of their sin.

This angered the people to the point that they convinced the Roman governor to crucify Him. The raging crowd had its base instincts satisfied by seeing Jesus beaten, spit on, whipped, crowned with thorns, mocked, taunted, and nailed to the cross. Finally, it seemed that He who had claimed to be the Son of God, sent by God to die for the sin of the world, the One who stirred up the rulers by exposing their hypocrisy and pricking their consciences, was removed.

No sooner did He die, than God shook the earth and caused the rocks to split. The precise timing, location, and magnitude of this quake caused the echoing jeers of His persecutors,

> "Come down off the cross if you are the Son of God!"
> (Matthew 27:40)

to be replaced by the cry of the guards,

> "Surely He was the Son of God!" (27: 54)

When the British botanist F. Kingdon-Ward and his wife, Jean, witnessed rocks splitting during the 1950 Tibet earthquake, they considered it their most terrifying experience. Jean Kingdon-Ward commented, "The noise was unbelievable, agonizing. Never before had our ears been subjected to such an onslaught of sound." [1] They gained a realization of the mighty power emanating from an earthquake. In the case of the centurion and guards attending the crucifixion of Christ, they not only experienced the terrifying sight of an earthquake, but also became convinced that it was God— the Creator, the Source, and Initiator of the quake—who was confirming that Jesus was indeed the Son of God.

Resurrection

Only three days after Christ's burial, a second earthquake occurred in the immediate area.

> "Go make the tomb as secure as you know how." So they went and made the tomb secure by putting a seal on the stone and posting the guard.... (Matthew 27:65–66)

> ...After the Sabbath, at dawn on the first day of the week, Mary Magdalene and the other Mary went to look at the tomb. *There was a violent earthquake,* for an angel of the Lord came down from heaven and, going to the tomb, rolled back the stone and sat on it. (28:1–2)

The Jewish priests and scribes, remembering that Jesus had said He would rise from the dead after three days, convinced the Roman governor to order the tomb to be secured. Perhaps if the scribes had told the Roman guards about the God who shook Sinai, they would not have wasted their time on such a vain effort.

No matter how well the Roman governor may have secured the tomb, and no matter how well we may try to secure our buildings, as a structural engineer I know that we can design buildings to be earthquake *resistant*, but never 100% earthquake *proof*. If God ultimately chooses to move or destroy, it happens, regardless of man's feeble efforts to prevent it.

The Early Christians are Shaken

Two further events of a seismic nature are described in the book of Acts. The early Christians were being threatened for proclaiming that Jesus had risen from the dead and that it was Jesus' power which enabled them to perform miracles. During one instance, they gathered to pray that God would accompany their witness with miraculous signs and wonders in order to reinforce their proclamation of the gospel of Jesus. Then we read:

> After they prayed, the place where they were meeting was *shaken*. (Acts 4:31)

No sooner had they prayed, than the building shook. It was God's affirmation that He had heard their prayers. Rod Zook, a missionary with the organization New Tribes Missions, reports a similar experience in the video *"EE-Taow!"—The Next Chapter*. Just as he was teaching the recently-converted tribal Christians about this occurrence in Acts 4, the ground and canopy under which he was standing began to shake violently. He reports that the people remained calm, taking the entire matter in stride, as if to say: "Yes, that's just like our powerful God...."[2]

Earthquake Breaks the Chains of Prison

An interesting account is related in Acts 16, where two of the early Christians, Paul and Silas, find themselves imprisoned because of their missionary activities.

> After they had been severely flogged, they were thrown into prison, and the jailer was commanded to guard them carefully. Upon receiving such orders, he put them in the inner cell and fastened their feet in the stocks. About midnight Paul and Silas were praying and singing hymns to God, and the other prisoners were listening to them. Suddenly, there was such a *violent earthquake* that the foundations of the prison were shaken. At once all the prison doors flew open, and everybody's chains came loose. (Acts 16:23–26)

This description bears some resemblance to the resurrection earthquake, in that extra precautionary measures had been taken to guard Paul and Silas. They were put in the inner cell and fastened in stocks. While shifting foundations and opening doors are common occurrences during earthquakes, in this case the quake also loosened the chains of the prisoners. Furthermore, the jailer woke up, and upon seeing the open doors he immediately realized the grave consequences he would be facing for his failure to provide adequate supervision of the inmates. He decided to commit suicide instead. The narrative continues:

> But Paul shouted, "Don't harm yourself! We are all here!" The jailer called for lights, rushed in and fell trembling before Paul and Silas. He then brought them out and asked, "Sirs, what must I do to be saved?"

31

They replied, "Believe in the Lord Jesus Christ and you will be saved—you and your household." Then they spoke the word of the Lord to him and to all the others in his house....The jailer brought them to his house and set a meal before them, and the whole family was filled with joy, because they had come to believe in God. (Acts 16:28–32, 34)

This particular earthquake obviously triggered a most extraordinary turn of events.

Not unlike the experience of the jailer was the experience of Esterina Candela whose ordeal was described in the first chapter and who survived the 1980 earthquake in Italy. She describes in her own words the days following the earthquake:

"I remember running through the streets and crying. The earthquake caused me to think about my family, my life—what was the meaning of it all? I wanted to find the answer before another earthquake struck. I became very scared. I longed for assurance and security—so that I would be prepared to appear before God. If at all possible, I wanted to do something myself to achieve a measure of peace....I began to read the Bible....Thank God, our house was rebuilt (with the help of the government). However, the most special blessing I received as a result of the earthquake was coming to know the Lord Jesus Christ as my Savior. What ultimately will remain and always be mine are redemption from sin and salvation—this is much more important than our house."[3]

CHAPTER FOUR

EARTHQUAKES, PROPHECY AND THE BIBLE

Numerous passages in the Scriptures contain prophetic announcements regarding future earthquake activity. We will now look at several of these—not, however, with the intent of speculating on the precise dates and locations of future earthquakes. The purpose of such prophecy is not to enable mankind to incorporate earthquake preparedness programs in time for the *Big One*, nor to help futurists profit financially from speculative predictions. The real purpose of such prophetic statements will become evident in the course of our discussion.

Prophecies of Jesus

We begin by looking at the words of Jesus in the Book of Mark.

> Nation will rise against nation, kingdom against kingdom. And there will be *earthquakes* in various places and there will be famines and troubles. These are the *beginnings of sorrows*. (Mark 13:8 NKJV)

The parallel account in the Gospel of Luke refers to great earthquakes in various places (21:11) and heavenly bodies that will be shaken (21:26). In this prophetic passage, Jesus gives a partial answer to the question His disciples had just posed, namely, When would Jerusalem and its magnificent temple be destroyed (an event that Jesus had predicted earlier), what would be the signs of impending disaster, and when would the end of time come? In the minds of His disciples, the timing of the two events—the destruction of Jerusalem with its treasured temple and the end of the world—were synonymous. We know that Jesus' prophetic word was partially fulfilled during the total destruction of Jerusalem in A.D. 70, not by an earthquake, but by the Roman army led by Titus. We also know that the end of the world has not yet come.

The purpose of forewarning His disciples and future followers of impending earthquakes as well as other catastrophes—wars and famines—was to prevent them from concluding in the midst of such cataclysmic and earth-shattering occurrences that the end of the world was at hand. They were to remain calm and clear minded, not falling prey to the plethora of false prophets who would surely arise, declare themselves to be the Messiah, and pronounce the imminent demise of the world.

Many great earthquakes have happened during the past two thousand years. Surely, many a person has probably thought the end of the world was imminent, particularly when, for example, the death toll climbed to 830,000 people in the 1556 Shensi, China, earthquake.[1] Various people have professed to be the Messiah or a prophet predicting the end of all things; but none of these prophesies came true.

We should note at this point that God provided a very simple test by which mankind could recognize the true prophet sent by God, as opposed to the false prophets. If a prophet's pronouncement did not come true 100% of the time, then he was a false prophet. God's prophets were unerringly right 100% of the time.

Moses, for instance, prophesied about 3500 years ago that the Israelites would, because of their disobedience to God, be dispersed over the whole globe (Deuteronomy 28:64–68); and they were. He also predicted that, some time in the future, they would return to their homeland, Palestine (30:3–6). During the following millennia, nations and individuals alike, including Christians, scoffed at such a preposterous idea. But on May 15, 1948, the state of Israel was proclaimed. Once again, God's prophet was proven to be right.

Jesus, prophesying the events which would precede the end of all things, used the expression *beginning of sorrows* or *birth pains,* which suggests two things.

First, birth pains increase in frequency but also, more importantly, in intensity as the time of actual birth approaches. We can expect the number of earthquakes, wars, and other catastrophic events to increase. It is not possible

35

to statistically determine if there has been a gradual increase in the number of earthquakes worldwide during the past 2000 years. This is due to inadequate record keeping during earlier centuries. It should, however, be noted that lighter birth pains often occur very infrequently for a long period of time before culminating in a series of very intense pain cycles just prior to actual birth. There have been numerous major earthquakes during the past century. Likewise, the two most devastating wars in history also occurred during the last 100 years. It may very well be that these disasters are part of the intensifying birth pains the earth will experience.

What is abundantly clear is that the casualties, injuries, and damages caused by earthquakes have historically increased and have become more widespread as the population of the world continues to grow.

Recently a conference was convened bringing together experts from all the 80 Ring-of-Fire countries around the Pacific Ocean. According to Larry Pearce, executive director for the conference, the purpose of the gathering was to address what scientists say is a significant increase in natural disasters in the last 20 years. In fact, the 1990s have been declared the International Decade for Disaster Reduction (IDNDR).

While it is difficult to substantiate an increase in the number of disasters due to inadequate record keeping in earlier centuries, it is plainly evident that the impact of natural disasters is becoming much harsher due to the fact that highly vulnerable areas contain large population centers with expensive buildings and goods. Alan Davenport, chairman of the IDNDR, states, "Insurance companies are already concerned with the explosive increase in the number of natural disasters."[2]

What should also be noted is that *birth pains* or *travailing sorrows* also imply that earthquakes and disasters are giving birth to something new. This, in fact, as suggested by the context, is the kingdom of God and the ultimate renewal and rebirth of heaven and earth.

The Book of Revelation

We find many references to earthquakes in the last book of the Bible, the Book of Revelation. In this book, the writer, John, portrays the vision given to him by an angel of "what must soon take place" (Revelation 1:1). The general theme presents Jesus Christ's victory over Satan, His judgment of the godless and the ultimate redemption of the believers.

The following is a typical reference describing the awesome, majestic authority of Christ in the Book of Revelation:

> …And there came peals of thunder, rumblings, flashes of lightning and an earthquake. (Revelation 8:5)

In his vision, John sees these natural occurrences accompanying Christ's final judgment of the nations. Two passages of particular note are found in chapters 11 and 16.

> At that very hour there was a *severe earthquake* and a tenth of the city collapsed. Seven thousand people were killed in the *earthquake,* and the survivors were terrified and gave glory to the God of heaven. (11:13)

> Then they gathered the kings together to the place that in Hebrew is called Armageddon. The seventh an-

gel poured out his bowl into the air, and out of the temple came a loud voice from the throne, saying, "It is done!" Then there came flashes of lightning, rumblings, peals of thunder and a *severe earthquake.* No earthquake like it has ever occurred since man has been on earth, so tremendous was the quake. The great city split into three parts, and the cities of the nations collapsed. God remembered Babylon the Great and gave her the cup filled with the wine of the fury of His wrath. Every island fled away and the mountains could not be found. (16:16–20)

Although Bible expositors differ in their interpretations of the details in these passages, one thing becomes very clear: Earthquakes of tremendous magnitude will cause widespread collapse. The *city* or the *great city*, most probably Jerusalem, experiences both quakes described here while the entire world is affected by the most severe earthquake to ever shake this planet. *Babylon the Great* is a descriptive name symbolizing the godless nature of all men and women who have turned away from God—the Creator and Ruler of mankind and the whole universe—and who, instead, have chosen to serve their own corrupt instincts.

The statement, "Every island fled away and the mountains could not be found," implies incredible shifting of rock and soil taking place during the quake. A descriptive account of the 1811 Madrid, Missouri, earthquake reads as follows: "On the Mississippi, great waves were created...high banks caved and were precipitated into the river; sandbars and points of islands gave way; *and whole islands disappeared.*"[3]

Although the prophetic passage in Revelation could actually imply a total, physical disappearance of every mountain and island, it could also be interpreted as the reconfiguration of those elements on the earth's crust—somewhat like rearranging the pattern on a Rubik's cube. Perhaps this is the earthquake the Old Testament prophets Isaiah and Ezekiel spoke of when they wrote:

> The earth is *broken up*, the earth is *split asunder*, the earth is thoroughly *shaken*. The earth reels like a drunkard, it sways like a hut in the wind, so heavy upon it is the guilt of its rebellion, that it falls, never to rise again. (Isaiah 24:19–20)

> In My zeal and fiery wrath I declare that at that time there shall be a *great earthquake* in the land of Israel. The fish of the sea, the birds of the air, the beasts of the field, every creature that moves along the ground, and *all* people on the face of the earth will tremble at My presence. The mountains will be overturned, the cliffs will crumble and every wall will fall to the ground. (Ezekiel 38:19–20)

This final display on earth of God's wrath, awesome power, and majestic authority will catapult all those living on earth into a state of fear and trembling never before experienced by mankind.

CHAPTER FIVE

WHAT CAUSES THE EARTH TO TREMBLE?

Throughout the ages, many theories have been put forward to explain the ultimate cause of earthquakes. This is not surprising, in light of the fact that the whole earth has been trembling as long as man can remember.

Egyptian and Greek legends tell of the lost continent of Atlantis, which, thousands of years ago, disappeared into the sea overnight. Recent archaeological discoveries lend credence to this story.[1] Another giant earthquake is said to have shaken the area around the Mediterranean about 3000 B.C. and 2500 B.C., from Gibraltar to Turkey and from Greece to Egypt.[2] In China, there are records dating back to 780 B.C. that list what are thought to be all moderate to major earthquakes in central China around that time. Thus, the presence of earthquakes, coupled with an ever-increasing

41

awareness of them, has prompted many to philosophize about this unique phenomenon.

Ancient people developed different ideas to explain earthquakes. Some Native Americans blamed the movements of a great tortoise; the Mongolians thought the earth was shaken by a pig; and in India the culprit was a mole. The Japanese first blamed a spider, then the creature was surmised to be a catfish kept quiet by a rock on its head from which it tried to wriggle free.[3]

Inhabitants of the Kamchatka peninsula believed that earth tremors were caused by the dogs of the god Twil.[4] The 1819 Allah Bund earthquake in India credits its name to Allah as the creator of the fault or scarp that generated the seismic shock.

The famous Greek scientist and philosopher Aristotle (384–322 B.C.) proposed a more scientific theory. According to him, powerful winds circulated beneath the earth; and when they had nowhere to go, they broke through to the surface of the earth. This theory, by the way, seems to have been accepted even in the time of Shakespeare.[5]

Around that time, however, another explanation became current. It was thought that the collapse of huge, underground caverns were the cause of earthquakes.[6]

More recently, an earthquake jolted Vancouver, Canada, three hours after a speaker gave an earthquake-preparedness lecture to a women's gathering. The speaker joked afterward that she might have "called up the devil."

While many of these explanations may sound humorous in today's age, we cannot deny that there is a common tendency to ascribe the cause of earthquakes to a higher being. We should also take note of the fact that our western legal system refers to an earthquake as an "Act of God," while other people are satisfied with ascribing credit to Mother Nature as the mover of tectonic plates and the creator of faults.

While it is apparent that natural forces and laws are at work causing earthquakes, we see that ultimately it comes down to a question of *who*, rather than *what*, shakes the earth. Who, then, is the One that causes the earth to tremble? The answer to this question cannot be found by indulging in our imaginations or by simply pursuing scientific formulations. I suggest we turn to the Bible, where the One who ultimately shakes the earth is clearly identified.

The Creator

The Bible identifies Him as the Creator of the universe.

> He set the earth on its foundation....He looks at the earth, and it trembles; He touches the mountains, and they smoke. (Psalms 104:5, 32)

Here is a description from the Book of Job:

> He shakes the earth from its place and makes its pillars tremble...He alone stretches out the heavens and treads on the waves of the sea. He is the Maker of the Bear and the Orion, the Pleiades and the constellations of the south. He performs wonders that cannot be fathomed.... (Job 9:6, 8–10)

The truth is that, in spite of our already vast and ever-increasing knowledge of seismic phenomena, humans will never be able to fathom the vast powers which make the earth tremble.

The God of Israel

The Bible identifies the only true God as the God of Israel, the God of the Old Testament Jewish patriarchs—Abraham, Isaac, and Jacob—and the God of the Hebrew prophets. God elected Israel to be His chosen people so that through His dealings with this nation He might manifest His power, communicate His moral law, and show His love to the world. This became evident when He shook Mount Sinai with Moses and Israel gathered there to receive the Ten Commandments.

> The earth shook, the heavens poured down rain, before God, the One of Sinai, before God, the God of Israel. (Psalm 68:8)

The descriptions of earthquakes in the Old Testament clearly point to the God of Israel as the One who shakes the earth, causing, for instance, the Philistines—Israel's enemy—to panic. He is the One who quaked the earth beneath Elijah's feet in order to remind this downcast Jewish prophet that the God of Israel was still in control of all things—man and nature alike.

The Resurrected Christ

This Creator of the universe, the God of Israel, is also the One who has revealed himself in the person of Jesus Christ.

[Jesus] is the image of the invisible God, the first-born over all creation. *For by Him all things were created:* things in heaven and on earth, visible and invisible...*in Him all things hold together.* (Colossians 1:15–17)

The entire earth, with its mountains, valleys, shifting faults and tectonic plates, is held together at the command of Christ. This was most poignantly displayed during the crucifixion of Christ. As soon as He had uttered His last words and died, an earthquake of rock-splitting magnitude shook the ground, causing a guard to exclaim:

"Surely He was the Son of God!" (Matthew 27:54).

Nowhere was it more triumphantly proclaimed that it is Jesus who holds this trembling world in His hand than during the resurrection of Jesus from the dead. A violent earthquake ripped the seal from the tomb of Christ and rolled away the rock, only to reveal that the grave was empty. The Creator, the God of Israel, the Son of God, the Christ who died was, and is, alive!

CHAPTER SIX

WHY DOES THE CREATOR SHAKE THE EARTH?

Why, then, does the earth tremble, and for what purpose does God cause it to shake? The various earthquakes we have seen described in the Bible, the prophetic statements we have looked at, as well as other Scripture passages, help us find the answers to these questions and to better understand how God uses natural phenomena to achieve His purposes.

There are scientific explanations of why earthquakes happen. According to the plate-tectonics theory, the earth's surface consists of rigid plates, which slowly move past each other. This motion squeezes and stresses the edges of the plates. Once the force on the edges becomes too great, the rocks rupture and shift suddenly, causing earthquakes.

In Vancouver, geophysicists believe we are situated in a subduction zone, where the Juan de Fuca plate is sliding under the North American plate. It is thought that the leading edge of the top plate is being "caught up," or stuck, on the lower plate. Ultimately, the stress building up will reach a point where the toe of the North American plate will break loose and cause a massive earthquake.

Such occurrences are, on the one hand, natural phenomena like hurricanes, floods, and tornadoes. On the other hand, however, such explanations, while rational, fail to provide us with an answer as to the ultimate cause. Why should the earth's crust not remain completely static and stable? Why do some earthquakes, such as those mentioned in the Bible, occur with such pinpoint accuracy and timing so as to defy human explanation? Why would a loving God allow such disasters to happen?

There are several reasons why God shakes the earth.

Man's Rebellion

Earthquakes are the result of man's rebellion against God. Some may say this sounds really absurd. We read these insightful words in the Bible:

> For the creation was subjected to frustration, not by its own choice, but by the will of the One who subjected it, in hope that the creation itself will be liberated from its bondage to decay and brought into the glorious freedom of the children of God. We know that the whole creation has been *groaning as in the pains of childbirth* right up to the present time. (Romans 8:20–22)

What does this tell us? The Bible teaches that God created the first human beings—Adam and Eve—who rebelled against their Creator. Satan presented them with the prospect of becoming "like God" if they would eat of the forbidden fruit in the Garden of Eden. He assured them that in doing so, they *"would surely not die"* (Genesis 3).

It is no accident that many leaders of today's New Age movement teach the same two lies. The first lie tells us that we are not accountable to a higher authority and each one of us is a god. The second tells us that we do not really die. Wanting to be like God and independent of him, Adam and Eve, like many people today, rejected their loving Creator as the ultimate authority in their life and ate of the fruit.

This is what the Bible calls *sin*. It means living apart from our God and Creator, going our own way, rebelling against His moral authority, and not being thankful to Him for the untold good gifts He bestows upon us every day.

The consequences of sin have been devastating and of "seismic" proportions, not only for Adam and Eve, but for all of humanity. Lying, stealing, murder, sexual immorality, perversion, and the occult are just some of the results of this rebellion that have brought "groanings," such as, endless fear, sickness, grief, and death to the human race.

God, being a holy God in whose presence no sinful person can stand, pronounced the curse,

> "For dust you are, and to dust you will return" (Genesis 3).

As we well know, everyone of us, every created being, faces the sure prospect of death—some through accidents, others by sickness, and yet others in earthquakes.

However, what the verses in Romans 8 tell us is that, not only mankind, but *all* of God's creation was subjected to this curse, including plants and animals as well as the earth itself—not by its own choice, but rather by the will of God. So we find that nature, even the earth itself, *groans* for freedom from this curse. This is physically manifested in the earth literally quaking thousands of times a year and continuously trembling as it awaits the day that God will release His creation from the curse of sin.

A poem called *Earthquake*, written in 1750, summarizes this predicament:

> What powerful hand with force unknown
> Can these repeated tremblings make
> Or do the imprisoned vapours groan?
> Or do the shores with fabled Tridents shake?
> Ah no! the tread of impious feet
> The conscious earth impatient bears
> And shuddering with the guilty weight,
> One common grave for her bad race prepares.
> —*Anonymous*

The following verse describes the vision of the Hebrew prophet Isaiah:

> The earth is broken up, the earth is split asunder, the earth is thoroughly shaken. The earth reels like a drunkard, it sways like a hut in the wind; so heavy upon it is the guilt of its rebellion, that it falls—never to rise again. (Isaiah 24:19–20)

It is interesting to note that Jesus, when speaking to His disciples about future events, referred to the coming catastrophes, including earthquakes, as the beginning of *birth pains*. The previously quoted passage from the Book of Romans uses a similar description when it says, "The whole creation has been groaning as in the *pains of childbirth* right up to the present time."

Just as with the birth pains an expectant mother experiences, so the earth experiences tremors with ever-increasing intensity, finally yielding an earthquake that, according to Revelation 16, will be: "Such that no earthquake like it has ever occurred since man has been on earth, so tremendous [will be] the quake."

Why does the earth tremble? It quakes because it literally groans for release from the curse to which it was subjected when man rebelled and sinned against God.

Sign of God's Grace

God reveals His grace and mercy even in earthquakes. Strange as it may sound, earthquakes may be regarded as a safety measure—in particular, the millions of small ones the earth experiences every year that save us from far greater disasters. Small earthquakes release the stress and strain of the rocks until the titanic forces can no longer be dissipated by small tremors. We have reason to be thankful that, worldwide, only a relatively small number of major earthquakes strike each year.

It has been postulated that earthquake activity is also a sensitive parameter for life. Dr. Hugh Ross, an astrophysicist, writes in his book *The Creator and the Cosmos*:

> Without earthquakes, nutrients essential for life on the continents would erode and accumulate in the oceans.

However, if earthquake activity were too great, it would be impossible for humans to reside in cities. On earth, the number and intensity of earthquakes is large enough to recycle life-essential nutrients back to the continents but not so intense that dwelling in cities is impossible.[1]

God's grace can be seen in that there is a silver lining to this otherwise dark cloud called earthquakes, and that earthquakes, too, were designed by our all-wise Creator to help sustain life on this planet.

Confirmation of God's Word

God also uses earthquakes to reinforce His Word. It is interesting to note that the four pinnacles of biblical history are accompanied by earthquakes. First, God shook Mount Sinai when He descended upon it and gave Moses the Ten Commandments, clearly showing the Israelites that God was present. Second, the crucifixion of Jesus was immediately followed by a rock-splitting quake, convincing the guards that it was God who was at work. Third, the resurrection of Christ was accompanied by an earthquake that tore the seal from the tomb, leaving no doubt in the minds of the guards as to who had rolled away the stone. Fourth, in the Book of Revelation, we read that, at the end of time and the gathering of the nations' kings at Armageddon, God will make His power abundantly evident with the most severe earthquake ever to shake the earth.

We also read in Acts 4 that God shook the building where the Christians were praying to confirm that His power would accompany their message. It reminds me of an experience Pastor Wilhelm Busch had in Germany roughly 40 years ago. One of his former professors asked him to preach at a gathering in the city of Tübingen. The professor, being quite ill, stayed at home. The first evening, Pastor Busch began his sermon by relating an encounter he had had the same day with a young student. The student had insisted that with respect to such matters as having security here on earth, his feet were, so to speak, planted on "solid ground." The pastor asked him, "Don't you realize, though, that the ground beneath you is shaky?"

No sooner had Pastor Busch related this experience to a packed audience in the church than a moderate earthquake suddenly jolted the structure, causing the lights to go out. Fearing the crowd might break out in a panic, he continued preaching in the dark until some candles were brought in. A while later, when the pastor was visiting the sick professor, he told him about his experience. The professor replied, "Every evening at eight o'clock, when you stepped into the pulpit, I prayed for you."

Those present that evening recognized the earthquake as a confirmation that God was reinforcing the message of his servant, Pastor Busch.[2]

Judgment

Earthquakes have sometimes been used by God as a specific act of judgment. We have read the account of the rebellion against Moses in Numbers 16, when the earth literally swallowed up the guilty insurrectionists. Similarly, the most severe earthquake that will ever happen, as outlined in Revelation 16, is clearly an act of God's judgment on impenitent nations and their people.

> God remembered Babylon the Great and gave her
> the cup filled with the fury of His wrath. (Revelation
> 16:19)

It will be a most terrifying time for all inhabitants of the
world when God shakes the earth one more time.

Can we conclude, then, that all destructive earthquakes
are specific judgments for wrongdoing committed by nations or individuals? Earthquakes always have and will con-
tinue to cause deaths. In a general sense, they execute the
judgment of God by returning man "from dust to dust."
However, the timing and reasons for God's specific judgments on earth remain a secret. In ancient Israel, God announced specific judgments through the Hebrew prophets. Christ announced it, and the Bible describes the judgment awaiting us at the end of time. In the interim, we are
not given any specific reasons for judgment with respect to
modern-era earthquakes, except that they, too, are consequences of mankind's original rebellion against God—its
Creator.

When the 1989 Loma Prieta earthquake struck San
Francisco's Candlestick Park, a World Series baseball game
was immediately brought to a halt. A clock tower in Santa
Cruz ceased to function at 5:04 p.m. These are solemn re-
minders that life and time on this earth will also come to an
end someday.

On one occasion, Jesus spoke to His listeners about a
water tower that had collapsed at a place called Siloam,
killing eighteen people. He asked His listeners if they
thought the eighteen people who died were more guilty
than all the others living in Jerusalem. Jesus, in answering
His own question, then said,

"I tell you, no! but unless you repent, you too will all perish!" (Luke 13:4–5).

In other words, when natural disasters strike, they should not be interpreted as necessarily representing God's punishment for the worst sinners or most sinful cities. Nonetheless, we should let earthquakes remind us of our need to repent of our sins and of the fact that a final judgment day awaits us.

In the Book of Hebrews, written to the early Jewish Christians, the writer awakened their memory of the shaking of Mount Sinai to remind them of pending judgment:

> See to it that you do not refuse Him who speaks. If [Israel] did not escape when they refused Him who warned them on earth, how much less will we, if we turn away from Him who warns us from heaven. At that time His voice shook the earth, but now He has promised, "Once more will I shake not only the earth but also the heavens." (Hebrews 12:25–26)

Whether the earth trembles lightly or strongly, we are wise to let those tremblings serve as a solemn reminder of the coming judgment when God will shake not only the earth, but also the heavens. This leads us to another reason why God shakes the earth.

A Symbol of Things Unseen

On certain occasions, God chooses to shake created things—namely the earth—while at the same time shaking the heavens—those things that are invisible. Two passages in the Bible, one in the Old and one in the New Testament, make this connection very clear.

Looking back on the Sinai experience and awaiting the coming of Christ, the prophet Haggai wrote in the Old Testament:

> This is what the Lord Almighty says: "In a little while I will once more *shake* the heavens and the earth, the sea and the dry land. I will shake all nations...." (Haggai 2:6)

The Book of Hebrews in the New Testament, on the other hand, was written after the birth, death, and resurrection of Christ. In the previous chapter, we already mentioned part of the passage in Hebrews that refers to the prophecy in Haggai. It goes on to explain:

> At that time His voice shook the earth, but now He has promised, "Once more I will shake not only the earth but also the heavens." The words "once more" indicate the *removing* of that which can be shaken—that is, created things—so that what *cannot* be shaken may remain." (Hebrews 12:26–27)

When God shook Sinai, He also shook the invisible world—the corrupt moral order of the day—and gave the world the Ten Commandments, and thus a new moral code. The goodness and greatness of this law is demonstrated by the fact that all modern civilizations have built their code of ethics upon it.

When God shook the earth following the crucifixion of Christ, He also shook things invisible. Christ, by His own death on the cross, defeated Satan and overcame the power of sin. When God shook the earth during the resurrection of Christ, He shook the invisible world by declaring His ultimate victory over death. Finally, when God shakes the world at the end of time, He will also shake the invisible world by executing His final judgment and by establishing Christ's eternal kingdom.

So we find that, at times, God signifies and confirms the shaking of invisible things by physically shaking the earth at the same time. In all this, God desires to make us aware of our greatest need.

Our Need

Earthquakes show us that we need God! One of the most noticeable consequences of strong earthquakes is the awe survivors experience, as well as a personal sense of total insignificance. Reflecting on the devastating February 20, 1835 earthquake in Concepcion, Chile, Charles Darwin said,

> "A bad earthquake at once destroys the oldest associations; the world, the very emblem of all that is solid, had moved beneath our feet like a crust over a fluid; one second of time has created in the mind a strong idea of insecurity, which hours of reflection would not have produced."[3]

When God displays even a fraction of His awesome power by shaking the earth, not only is man inspired with an overwhelming sense of awe, but he also experiences the words of the Psalmist:

O Lord,…what is man that You are mindful of him,
the son of man that You care for him? (Psalm 8:4)

Earthquakes shake all our own ideas of earthly security
to the core—ideas about money, possessions, and philoso-
phy. This results in a sense of total helplessness and in feelings of complete insecurity, which, in turn, lead to fear and
despair. The Kingdon-Wards, botanists working in Tibet,
together with their servants experienced this helplessness
during the 1950 Assam, Tibet, earthquake. All four lay on
the earth, face down, gripping each other's hand.

> We waited in indescribable terror for the enraged
> earth to open beneath us and swallow us whole. It seemed
> impossible that any of us could escape that fate, for the
> convulsions beneath us never ceased for minutes on end;
> and how long, I wondered, could the tortured sand bear
> our weight upon it? Helpless as we were in the grip of
> the earthquake, every one of us, I think, experienced that
> night the uttermost depths of human fear.[4]

How can this possibly have any beneficial value?
We have already seen in Acts 16 what effect the earthquake had on the jailer. Prior to the earthquake, he had a
secure position; immediately following, he became totally
frightened and insecure—facing the prospect of losing his
job as well as his life. After being dissuaded by Paul and
Silas—his two most important prisoners—from commit-
ting suicide, he fell down before them, trembling and crying out,

"Sirs, what must I do to be saved?" (Acts 16:30)

We can observe how God used the earthquake to achieve His purpose; the heart of the jailer was prepared to receive the comforting words of the gospel:

> Believe on the Lord Jesus Christ and you will be saved—you and your household! (Acts 16:31)

Paul and Silas went on to explain to him and his whole family who Christ was, that He was sent by God to die as a sacrifice for the sin of the world, and that He arose from the dead. The final result was that the jailer placed His faith and trust in Christ as his Savior, and:

> The whole family was filled with joy, because they had come to believe in God. (Acts 16:34)

He also retained his job, while Paul and Silas were ordered to be released the next day.

Hardship and difficulty, pain and suffering, disappointment and hopelessness are things we all experience at one time or another. However, God uses such times to shake us loose from our devices of earthly security and remind us of our sinful, utterly helpless condition and our need for a savior. The Bible teaches that those who, in their brokenness and despair, humbly turn to God for help will experience His mercy and favor.

> He heals the brokenhearted and binds up their wounds....The Lord delights in those who fear Him, who put their hope in His unfailing love. (Psalm 147:3, 11)

This was the experience of Esterina Candela, survivor of the 1980 Italian earthquake.

Following the Armenian earthquake on December 7, 1988, many social agencies from western countries supplied this area of devastation with relief. When a spokesman for a Christian relief agency was asked what item was in greatest demand, he replied, "Bibles." Interesting that in light of the destruction of so many homes, people are crying out for Bibles. We are so prone to place our security in earthly things. However, the experience of an earthquake can, in a moment, remind us of what little security our earthly possessions offer us.

In many instances, God's mercy reaches us on the wings of suffering and His gift of forgiveness and new life is accompanied by the birth pains of personal loss. This suffering finds its climax in the sacrifice of the Son of God, as we read in the Book of Hebrews:

> Just as man is destined to die once, and after that to face judgment, so Christ was sacrificed once to take away the sins of many people; and He will appear a second time, not to bear sin, but to bring salvation to those who are waiting for Him. (Hebrews 9:27–28)

Out of the ashes of Christ's sacrifice rises the glorious hope of salvation.

Have you trusted in Him as your Savior? Are you waiting for Him?

A true story is told of whales that became trapped by ice in a bay along the northern coast of Siberia. Upon becoming aware of their plight, the Soviet navy sent icebreakers into the area in order to break open a path of escape. After creating a channel through which the enormous animals could swim, the whales, having been frightened by the drone of helicopters and sea vessels, refused to swim through the channel to open waters.

Because whales respond favorably to certain types of music, loudspeakers were set up on the deck of the ship. Various pieces of rock, jazz, and country music were played in an attempt to lure the whales from captivity. The whales did not respond. However, when the whales heard the harmonious and impassioned strains of Beethoven's Fifth Symphony, they swam through the path carved by the icebreaker and into the wide, open waters of freedom.

Here we have a picture of salvation! Humanity is trapped by the icy coldness of sin—with no way of escape. Jesus Christ, the Son of God, was bruised and beaten to death to create a pathway back to the vast, open waters of peace, harmony, and fellowship with our Creator. Our ears perceive those gentle, loving strains of the Savior's invitation.

> Come! And let him who hears say, "Come!" Whoever is thirsty, let him come; and whoever wishes, let him take the free gift of the water of life. (Revelation 22:17)

CHAPTER SEVEN

PREPARING FOR THE BIG ONE

I once read the passage in Revelation 16 describing the coming "most severe" earthquake to an architectural client during his visit to my office. Because we live on the west coast of Canada and find ourselves in a relatively high-risk seismic zone, he promptly asked the question, "If, in fact, there is such a massive earthquake coming, why bother incorporating seismic designs in our buildings?"

It was a good question that deserved a good response. In a more general sense, one may even ask, "How should we prepare for earthquakes, and how should we respond to what the Bible teaches us about earthquakes?"

There is a unique building in Vancouver, Canada, designed by my former employer Boguslav Babicki. It is supported by cables from a central concrete shaft. By virtue of its novel suspension design, it somehow gained the reputation amongst the lay population of Vancouver as being an earthquake-proof building. Even its designer would never call it that. It is true that even the famous architect, Frank Lloyd Wright, when working on his plans for the Imperial Hotel in Tokyo, expressed the opinion, "And I believed I could show them how to build an earthquake-proof masonry building."[1]

The fact of the matter is today we know that it is impossible to design a 100% earthquake-proof building for a worst-case scenario earthquake. Our experience with the 1995 Kobe, Japan, earthquake has reminded the design and research community not to become overly confident. Nevertheless, we can employ various measures to prepare for such potential disasters and mitigate risk.

Here are four principles to adhere to when preparing for earthquakes. They apply both to our physical as well as spiritual life and well-being.

Build on Solid Ground

Earthquake history has clearly taught us that the risk of experiencing destruction is substantially increased when we build on areas of landfill and loose sand. The recent 1995 Kobe, Japan, and 1989 Loma Prieta, California, earthquakes have abundantly demonstrated this. Alexander Pope, in *An Essay on Man*, writes: "He who builds his house on sand deserves a fool's cap." In San Francisco, after three previous earthquakes in 1864, 1898, and 1900, people had not stopped erecting houses and office buildings on land that had been filled in, as well as on reclaimed marshes and other wetlands.[2]

During my visit to San Francisco following the 1989 Loma Prieta earthquake, I observed that one of the most heavily damaged areas was the Marina District, which was built on landfill jutting out into the bay.

Similarly, Concepcion, Chile, has been razed by earthquakes five times in its history. After each devastation, a new city has been built on the rubble of the old.[3] After the initial terror, people disregard the earthquake and carry on with their lives as before.

This attitude mirrors man's approach in the spiritual realm. Human philosophies and ideas of security are giant spiritual landfills. When the great tribulations come, they give way and leave their believers in despair and destruction. Yet, how often we still insist on returning to that same heap of rubble—the same ideas that have proved unreliable and disastrous before.

Jesus taught the following about wise and foolish builders:

> "Why do you call me, 'Lord, Lord,' and do not do what I say? I will show you what he is like who comes to Me and hears My words and puts them into practice. He is like a man building a house, who dug down deep and laid the foundation on rock. When a flood came, the torrent struck that house but could not shake it, because it was well built. But the one who hears My words and does not put them into practice is like a man who built a house on the ground without a foundation. The moment the torrent struck that house, it collapsed and its destruction was complete." (Luke 6:46–49)

As a structural engineer, I have observed over the years that poor ground conditions are one of the most common causes of structural problems in buildings. How much more is this also true in the spiritual realm.

The first principle, then, of a wise builder is to build on solid ground—on Jesus Christ.

Strengthen Your House

Past earthquake experience and technological research have provided us with a wealth of knowledge for designing structures that will resist most earthquakes. For example: A homeowner can minimize earthquake hazards by incorporating such simple measures as bolting his house to the foundation, nailing plywood sheathing to exterior walls, securing cabinets and heavy furniture to the walls, and bracing brick chimneys. Houses constructed using these methods fared very well during the recent Kobe, Japan, earthquake. On the contrary, houses constructed using the traditional post and beam construction experienced widespread collapse.

I recall driving through a residential district of Santa Cruz with a colleague of mine following the Loma Prieta earthquake. We observed that some of the houses with poor crawlspace construction were leaning quite severely. I commented to my colleague that it would be wise for the homeowner to immediately nail plywood to the exterior walls to strengthen the house against potential aftershocks. No sooner had I spoken these words, when we noticed one homeowner who was strengthening his house in precisely this manner.

The question arises: How can we strengthen our spiritual house?

In Psalms we read:

"Unless the Lord builds the house, its builders labor in vain" (Psalm 127:1).

There is a maxim in the engineering community: If there is a weakness in the building, the earthquake will find it. In other words, earthquakes tend to shake buildings until they have found and exploited the weak link in the chain that will trigger the collapse of the structure.

In a similar manner, the experiences and circumstances of life have a tendency to exploit our human weaknesses. We are all exposed to the upheavals of life—our marriages are shaken, our jobs are threatened, our businesses subjected to unexpected pressures. Some people buckle under marriage pressures, others cave in under financial pressures. Amidst all these unpredictable circumstances, we build our lives in pursuit of security, happiness, and peace of mind.

Strengthening our spiritual house by trusting in Jesus Christ and "casting all our cares on Him" (1 Peter 5:7) will stabilize us, thus preparing us for the storms of life that will inevitably descend upon us.

Stock Up on Emergency Supplies

A common post-earthquake problem is a lack of water, heat, medical aid, and food. Earthquakes and the large earth movements associated with them often cause pipes to rupture and fires to break out. In fact, a large proportion of earthquake damage is often attributed to fire. The fires caused by the 1923 Tokyo earthquake raged for three days and gutted 65% of Tokyo's buildings.[4] Road and bridge damage typically hinders emergency vehicle access and food transport. Many people are left homeless as their houses have collapsed or are unsafe to live in.

People living in high-risk earthquake zones are therefore advised to purchase earthquake survival kits which may include such items as bottled water, imperishable food, first-aid items, flashlights, all season clothing and tents. Battery-operated radios, fuel, and emergency generators are other items that are useful for post-earthquake survival. A small investment beforehand can yield large returns in the time of emergency.

It is always difficult to spend money today on items that may not be required until some possibly distant time in the future. Nevertheless, wisdom often prevails, and we make the necessary sacrifices.

This third principle also applies to the spiritual realm. We can spend a lifetime selfishly pursuing financial security and earthly ambitions with no regard for God's counsel:

> Do not store up for yourselves treasures on earth, where moth and rust destroy, and where thieves break in and steal. But store up for yourselves treasures in heaven, where moth and rust do not destroy, and where thieves do not break in and steal. For where your treasure is, there your heart will be also. (Matthew 6:19–21)

I am reminded of an archaeological discovery vividly portraying the futility of placing our security in earthly possessions. It is the skeleton of a person, apparently caught by surprise by an earthquake, whose arm is stretched out toward some coins—but they are just beyond reach.

Doesn't this represent many of us? We spend a lifetime chasing earthly security, never becoming completely satisfied, always finding that the peace and contentment we seek remains elusive and just beyond our grasp.

We are wise if we trust in Jesus Christ and thus invest in eternal values.

Get Earthquake Insurance

It is possible that we may have built our house on solid ground, strengthened it as best we could, and stocked up on emergency items—but still get swallowed up or washed away by a *Big One*. In the event that we survive, the insurance industry would advise us of the prudence of purchasing earthquake insurance beforehand. This again, of course, incurs additional expense and in some areas, such as California, substantial expense. Nevertheless, most people in high-risk earthquake zones will purchase insurance to cover the potential loss of their home, contents, and business.

The Bible clearly teaches that there is a Big One coming, not only the most severe physical earthquake to ever occur, which is spoken of in Revelation 16, but more importantly, a spiritual *Big One*.

>...It is appointed for men to die once, but after this the judgment.... (Hebrews 9:27 NKJV)

All of mankind is guilty of sin and awaits this dreadful day.

>There is no one righteous, not even one....All have turned away. (Romans 3:10, 12)

Furthermore, there is nothing we can do within our own ability to prepare for this day. No amount of good works, church attendance, giving to the poor, living by the Golden Rule, or penance will absolve us of our guilt. This is an "earthquake" that no one can avoid. However, God offers us insurance in Christ Jesus.

> If we confess our sins, He is faithful and just and will forgive us our sins and cleanse us from all unrighteousness. (1 John 1:9)

> For it is by grace you have been saved, through faith—and this not from yourselves, it is the gift of God not by works, so that no one can boast. (Ephesians 2:8–9)

The gift of forgiveness can be received by all people who are willing to confess their sin and who decide to put their trust in Jesus to forgive their sin. The Old Testament prophet Nahum had a vision of the earth in the grip of God's judgement and wrath. However, he also recognized the overarching, radiant rainbow of His mercy and love.

> The mountains quake before Him and the hills melt away. The earth trembles at His presence, the world and all who live in it. Who can withstand His indignation? Who can endure His fierce anger? His wrath is poured out like fire; the rocks are shattered before Him. The Lord is good, a refuge in times of trouble. He cares for those who trust in Him. (Nahum 1:5-7)

Trusting in Jesus not only provides us with a place of refuge and peace of mind in the midst of judgement, but also gives us the assurance of a glorious, indescribably wonderful future in heaven.

> No eye has seen, nor ear heard, no mind has conceived what God has prepared for those who love Him. (1 Corinthians 2:9)

According to the Bible, those who choose to reject this gracious offer of forgiveness and salvation await a terrible end.

> He will punish those who do not know God and do not obey the Gospel of our Lord Jesus. They will be punished with everlasting destruction and shut out from the presence of the Lord and from the majesty of His power. (2 Thessalonians 1:8–9)

Several years ago, a landmark office tower in downtown Vancouver, Canada, was demolished to make way for a modern skyscraper. The existing building was demolished by means of implosion. Explosives were attached to critical support columns, and the surrounding streets were cordoned off.

Early on a Sunday morning, with the streets cleared and large crowds watching from a distance, the charges were detonated, and the building collapsed on itself. As the dust settled and the onlookers rushed forward to take a closer look at the remains, a most astonishing sight unfolded before my eyes. There, at the main viewing corner, perched in an upright position halfway up the mound of rubble and having survived all the cascading tons of concrete crashing down around it, was a sheet of plywood. Written on it were the large, bold letters: JESUS SAVES.

And so it is that through all the centuries of human despair, God has continued to allow the earth to shudder with earthquakes in order to shake and shatter our own notions of security. All the while, however, He has never ceased to beckon us with the unchanging, glorious message of Jesus Christ.

How should we then respond? Believe in the Lord Jesus Christ, and you will be saved!

END NOTES

Chapter One

1. Esterina Candela, *Tape Recorded by Paul Minder* (1991). Transcribed and translated into English (n.p.).
2. Henry Gilfond, *Disastrous Earthquakes* (New York/ London/ Toronto/ Sydney: A First Book, 1981), 58.
3. *The World Book Encyclopedia*, 1988 Edition
4. Gilfond, *Disastrous Earthquakes*, 45.
5. Ibid., 45–47.
   Bruce A. Bolt, *Earthquakes: A Primer* (San Francisco: W. H. Freeman and Company 1978), 7.
6. Carl Charlson. *Earthquake* (Boston WGBH/ Hamburg NDR Video production for NOVA, Cat. No. 9989, 1990) Gilfond, *Disastrous Earthquakes*, 55–56.
   Bolt, *Earthquakes: A Primer*, 151.
7. Gilfond, *Disastrous Earthquakes*; 32, 34, 53–55.
   Frank W. Lane, *The Elements Rage* (Philadelphia and New York: Chilton Books, A Division of Chilton Company Publishers, 1965), 217.
8. *The Vancouver Sun* (January and February 1995).
9. Frank Lloyd Wright, *Frank Lloyd Wright Collected Writings: Vol. 2* (Frank Lloyd Wright Foundation, Rizzoli

International Publications Inc., 1992), 259.

10. N. Raeburn, *Frank Lloyd Wright: Writings and Buildings* (Frank Lloyd Wright Foundation, New York: Horizon Press, 1960), 199.

11. Wright, *Frank Lloyd Wright Collected Writings: Vol. 2,* 264.

12. Raeburn, *Frank Lloyd Wright: Writings and Buildings,* 201.

13. Ibid., 206.
   Gilfond, *Disastrous Earthquakes*; 33, 39, 52.

14. Charlson, *Earthquake.*
   Bolt, *Earthquakes: A Primer,* 148–151.

15. Charlson, *Earthquake.*
   Bolt, *Earthquakes: A Primer,* 151.

16. Charlson, *Earthquake.*

17. Frank W. Lane, *The Elements Rage,* 227–228.
   Gilfond, *Disastrous Earthquakes,* 52.

Chapter Two
1. Bolt, *Earthquakes: A Primer,* 215–217.
2. Lane, *The Elements Rage,* 207–208.
3. Ibid., 208.
4. Amos Nur & Chris MacAskill, *The Walls Came Tumbling Down—Earthquakes in the Holy Land*; 47.6 min. (Stanford, CA: ESI Productions, 1991).
5. Lane, *The Elements Rage,* 227–228.
6. Pierre Berton, *A History of the Niagara Falls* (Toronto, Ontario: McClelland & Stewart Inc., 1992), 86–87.

Chapter Three
1. Lane, *The Elements Rage,* 211.
2. Rod Zook, *"EE-Taow"—The Next Chapter* (Sanford, FL:

Video by Destination Summit, New Tribes Mission, 1993).
3. Candela, *Tape Recorded by Paul Minder*.

Chapter Four
1. Gilfond, *Disastrous Earthquakes*, 45.
2. *The Vancouver Sun* (July 29, 1996), B1–2.
3. Nicholas Hunter Heck, *Earthquake History of the United States*; revised edition (through 1956) by R. A. Eppley, Washington, D.C.: U.S. Government Printing Office (No. 41–1).

Chapter Five
1. Gilfond, *Disastrous Earthquakes*, 17–18, 43.
2. Ibid., 43–44.
3. Lane, *The Elements Rage*, 201.
4. Ibid.
5. Ibid.
   Gilfond, *Disastrous Earthquakes*, 16.
6. Gilfond, *Disastrous Earthquakes*, 16.

Chapter Six
1. Hugh Ross, *The Creator and the Cosmos* (Colorado Springs, CO: Nav Press, 1995), 137.
2. Wilhelm Busch, *Plaudereien in meinem Studierzimmer* (Gladbeck/Westfalen: Schriftenmissions-Verlag, 1965), 19–20.
3. Bolt, *Earthquakes: A Primer*, 19.
4. Lane, *The Elements Rage*, 211.

Chapter Seven
1. Raeburn, *Frank Lloyd Wright: Writings and Buildings*, 199.

2. Gilfond, *Disastrous Earthquakes*, 48.
3. Lane, *The Elements Rage*, 218.
4. Gilfond, *Disastrous Earthquakes*, 39.

To order additional copies of

When the Earth Trembles

send $8.95 US + $3.95 shipping and handling to:

WinePress Publishing
PO Box 1406
Mukilteo, WA
98275

To order by phone,
please have your credit card ready and call

1-800-917-BOOK